Be Open

How to Unlock Your Heart to Discover God's Purpose for Your Life

Dr. Tony Williams

The Divine Design Series

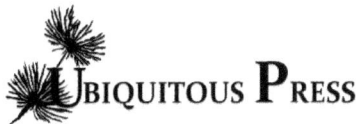

UBIQUITOUS PRESS

Morgan Hill, CA

Table of Contents

Foreword

Too many times the limits we place on God in our lives are colored by our own assumptions. We have confined the ways He can use us, how He speaks to us, the ways we are able to encounter Him and really know Him intimately. But the truth is that God is never limited by our narrow thinking or beliefs. The Aramaic word *Ephphatha* is found in the New Testament in Mark 7:34. It's translated as "be opened." I have discovered, after forty-five years of walking with the Lord in ministry, that "being open" is key to a thriving and growing relationship with Him.

Many times He speaks and deals with us in ways outside of the boxes we have attempted to place Him in. We find this to be true throughout the Scriptures. He calls Abraham and Sarah, who are childless and advanced in age, to birth a nation. He uses Moses, a foster child, to lead His people out of slavery. And He raises up a teenager named David to slay a giant.

As the Scripture says: "His ways are past finding out" (Rom. 11:33 KJV). In the New Testament He defies our logic when He uses a rough, uneducated fisherman to reach educated Jews and a Jewish scholar to reach out to uninformed Gentiles. His teachings virtually instruct us that the way up is down and to be first you must be last.

There are many other examples in Scripture that drive home the lesson that in our dealings with God we must at all times remain open to His unique ways. My hope is that in this book, by unfolding scriptural insights into what it means to be open, you will understand how to open the door to God so He might work in your life and you will recognize His work. My prayer is that your heart be open to the fresh and diverse ways that God uses to encounter and guide us through life.

Ephphatha! Be open!

~ Dr. Tony Williams, 2018

Introduction

There are many today searching for their purpose and calling in life. They truly want to hear from God, to know His mind and get His direction. But all too often they are "closed up" to hearing from God because of preconceptions that put Him in a box. To be open to hearing God's voice in our lives, we have to study the Scriptures to know both Him and His ways. If we fail to do so, we may miss His voice.

I personally believe in the principle of one "true calling." The better we understand this principle, the better we are able to distinguish our purpose and true calling as we open ourselves to hearing God's voice.

The principle is found in Mark 3:13–15 (NKJV):

> And He went up on the mountain, and He called to Him those He Himself wanted, and they came to Him. And He appointed twelve, that they might be with Him and that He might send them out to preach, to have power to heal sickness, and to cast out demons.

The principle I want to point out is that our calling is to *Him and to Him alone*—nothing and no one else.

I know it sounds a little like semantics, but the truth of the matter is, I was not called to preach, I was not called to prison work, I was not called to teach. I was called to *Him*.

Our calling is to Him. We see this as the twelve gather to hear Him. He called them to Himself, and they came to Him. And He appointed or ordained that they should "be with Him." And from His presence, He sent them out to fulfill their purpose.

He gave them power to heal sickness, power to cast out devils, power to teach, power to preach, power to do all the many wonderful things that God purposes for His people. But just as He instructed His disciples when He sent them out, when we get through fulfilling what He has sent us to do, we are always to return to His presence.

For those of you who are just beginning in ministry, or who feel a calling or a heart for ministry, you must understand and realize this truth—because it's the way to prevent burnout. You ask anyone who has been in ministry for some time—burnout can literally suck the life right out of ministry. We can get so burned out that we forget why we came to Christ in the first place.

I was thinking the other day how I'd been in ministry for forty-plus years, and I was feeling kind of discouraged, so I told the Lord, "You know, I didn't sign on for this. I didn't get saved for this." I thought back many years ago to when I first came to Christ. At that time I had desperate needs in my life: I needed deliverance, I needed salvation, and I needed direction, but when I came to Him, I simply fell in love with Jesus. As time went on, I went into ministry and got busy, involved in service and doing all the things that believers have opportunity to do, but I continually needed to remind myself how and why I got here in the first place.

His calling is always to Himself first and foremost. We go out and we preach and we teach, and we do all the things that God has given us to do, but when we have completed what He sent us to do, we need to come back to be with Him and to be filled again. And then He sends us out again.

But many times here's where the trouble starts. We go out in ministry and we stay out. We get burned out, and we get frustrated with people.

If you are going to work in ministry, you had better learn how to love people. Someone once said, "Church would be wonderful if it wasn't for the people."

We love the preaching and the teaching part. But then we get discouraged by all the problems, the pressures, the conflicting personalities, and the burden of administrative tasks and responsibilities. And if we forget that our calling is to be with Him, we will tire out and become soured on ministry. And that leads to becoming cynical, hard-hearted, narrow-minded, and legalistic, causing us to then miss out on the joy of ministry, the joy of serving God, the joy of knowing Him, the joy of spending a lifetime in His presence.

Jesus called His disciples to Himself for this purpose: that they might *be* with Him. And then He sent them out to heal the sick, to cast out devils, to bring deliverance, to preach the message of good news, and to do all the wonderful things that He purposed and gifted them to do.

He does the same with us. But when we get through, we must always return to Him.

Dr. Tony Williams

Part I: Positioning Ourselves to Hear God's Voice

Have you ever wondered if God is speaking to you? How can you know?

We don't have to guess or wonder if we are hearing God's voice. He tells us how to listen, how to prepare ourselves—our hearts, our minds, and our lives—in order to distinguish His voice from all others. God wants to speak to us, but we have to position ourselves so that we can hear Him. We have to unlock our hearts to discover God's purpose for our lives.

We have to "be opened!"

Chapter 1: Purpose Keeps Us from Spinning Our Wheels

One of the reasons it is so important to understand our purpose and understand His design for our lives is so we don't waste valuable time fulfilling His will for our lives. So we don't spin our wheels or put forth a lot of energy, a lot of time, and a lot of effort and not experience results in our lives. His *will* is the product that He has given us to produce.

So we must begin to look at ourselves as a whole and get an idea of how God made us.

How did God design you? How did God put you together? Why are you where you are? Why are you from the family that you are from? Why do you look like you look?

We ask questions like: "Why is my nose so big?" "Why don't I have any ankles?" "How come I wasn't gifted to be a great athlete and make millions of dollars?"

Instead of asking general questions that never truly get answered, I need to find what gifts have been deposited in me, because no one can beat me at being me. So I might as well begin to accept and understand how God made me and what kind of design God has for my life.

But first, I need to learn how to listen when God speaks, so I can get the blueprints for my unique design.

How God Speaks to Us

How does God speak to us?

When I was a new Christian, I always wondered how God speaks to someone, because people were always saying, "You know, the Lord told me," or "The Lord told me to tell you," or "I woke up the other morning and the Lord said . . ."

I thought, how do they know? When people would stand in the church to prophesy, and would say, "Yea, I say unto thee . . ." and they would declare the will of God, and we would hear the prophetic voice of God uttered in the congregation, I would always wonder, "Now, how does God talk to them? Do they hear a voice? What does His voice sound like? Is it high-pitched? Is it thundering? Does it vibrate? How do they know to stand up and prophesy? Does God give them the whole prophecy at first? Do they know everything they are going to say? Is it written down somewhere? Do they have it on their sleeve like crib notes or something, or do they just speak out and it just comes? What do you mean, the Lord woke you up and was talking to you the other night? What kind of stuff is that? God never came in my room and said anything!"

I never heard an audible voice, so that got me to asking, "Well, God, how are you going to speak to me? How am I going to know that you want me to stand and prophesy? How do I know when I should say, 'Now, the Lord showed me this'? How do I know when you are speaking to me? It's wonderful how you speak to others. They have marvelous ministries. But, Lord, how are you going to use *me*? How am I going to know your voice? How am I going to know what to do? Is it going to be through trial and error? Am I going to make mistakes? Am I going to miss you?"

And a resounding "yes" was the answer to all those questions. And so I began this study more than two decades ago in divine design to see how I was made.

One of the things that brought me pleasure was working out. I needed to exercise, so I joined a gym for a couple of years but only went but one time. Then I was going to start jogging. So I bought the good-looking jogging shoes and a book on running; I was going to get out every morning. And I ran for a little while, and I thought, "This is lonely; I don't like to do this." So then I thought I would go swimming every morning and swim ten laps up and down at the Olympic pool, and afterward, when I headed out in the morning, I would be refreshed and ready to face my day. But the water was just too cold, and though I do love swimming, I saw that plan was not going to work.

Then I remembered that when I was a child, the one thing I loved to do in San Francisco was ride my bicycle. And so I bought a bicycle, and I got great joy from just riding my bicycle. That may seem like a small thing to you, but for me it was special. That was part of the design that God had for me. I was learning how to be who He designed me to be.

I can't be like anyone else. I can't shape my life after anyone else's ministry. I can't try to do what someone else has told me works for them. I need to find out what works for me, begin the joy of real relationship with the Lord with Him revealing to me how I'm made up and why I am like I am.

I needed to recognize that He had a design for my life. That He gave me sisters and a mom, and that where I grew up served to form me to become who God designed me to be, and none of my past was wasted, even though I'd spent many years addicted to drugs and in and out of a lot of trouble in my younger years. I would not be defined simply by my past. Instead, I understood God was using all my experiences in His master design.

What God showed me was that no experience is ever wasted and that He was going to use every day of my life for His purposes. That He was going to take gifts that I didn't even think I had and use them for His glory.

And I thought, "Gee, maybe I'll be in the singing ministry!" But when I tried that, someone said, "You know, brother, that's not your calling. Sorry." Then I thought maybe I'd play an instrument. "No, that's not your calling either, brother." I was confused. I thought, what can I do? Maybe I can teach kids to play athletics. Well, I wasn't that good at sports myself, so it didn't make sense to be teaching anyone else.

What was my purpose? I kept wondering. Well, maybe I'd be a great administrator and pull things together. No, that wasn't it either. I asked God: "What in the world can I do? How did you make me; what did you design me for?"

And this is what He told me: "*You know, the one thing you have that is your gift and your curse at the same time is your ability to talk. You have been talking all your life. You could hang on the street corners and talk all night long."*

"Talk?" I asked.

"Yes. I'm going to use that gift. Let me refine it. Let me hold it. Let me sanctify it. Let me turn it and mold it."

And so I have been gifted for forty-plus years to make my living by preaching and teaching and talking.

God takes those things He's deposited in us that sometimes we're not aware of and uses them for His glory.

Using the Gifts God Deposited in You

I know people who have far more gifts than I do. They play music, they sing, they write, they are authors, they can preach and speak. And, somehow, they don't use any of those gifts. See, it is not a matter of what you have; it is how you *use* what you have. It's the *way* you use what you have.

When I preach, I don't have to preach like T. D. Jakes. I don't have to preach like R. W. Schambach. I don't have to preach like Billy Graham. I have to communicate in the manner and the way that God has laid out for me.

When we start out, we try to emulate someone else. I wanted to be able to hold my Bible like Mr. Graham used to hold it. He used to say, "You know, the Bible says . . ." and he had such authority. And I wanted to preach with the energy of R. W. Schambach and the intensity of T. D. Jakes, but I realized I'd get hoarse in about fifteen minutes.

So we often start out emulating others, but that's not what God is after at all. God wants us to be ourselves, bring who we are to the table, so He can use that unique design for His purpose.

No Less Valuable Than Anyone Else

The next thing we need to recognize is that God is able speak to us just as clearly as He speaks to anyone else. God can use you and give you a revelation just as He can give one to anyone else. Your thoughts and the things that God reveals to you are just as valuable, just as valid, as anyone else's. You must take confidence in this as you begin to learn to hear from God for yourself.

God is seeking prophets. Not the sons of prophets. The sons of prophets hear what someone else says and they then go repeat it. But prophets hear from God and share His heart.

Hearing from God doesn't have to occur while behind a pulpit; it could be while you're playing with your children. It could be while you're on your job, and He tells you something you need to know about your environment. It could be about what you are going to do next in your life, what decisions and choices God has for you.

You need to hear from God and understand how God speaks to you and, after that, once God has spoken, to know how His will and purpose works in your life.

The Bible says, "Work out your own salvation with fear and with trembling, for it is God that works in you, both to do and to will His good pleasure" (Phil. 2:12 NKJV).

God works in us! We have all the gifts and abilities we need. We have all that God has deposited within us. And now it is our responsibility to work it out. We have all the power of heaven behind us. We have all the enlightening power of the Holy Spirit residing within us. We have the gifts of God, and He is backing us in everything that He has worked in us.

Head Knowledge Comes First

As God reveals His purposes, the first knowledge that we gain is head knowledge. We read the Word; we hear the Word preached and taught, and it reaches our head, and we understand it.

But head knowledge is really dead knowledge until it is transferred from the head to the heart. Some people miss God by eighteen inches. That's the distance from your brain to your heart.

Some people miss God completely. They're in the house, just like the older brother in the parable of the prodigal son—you remember he came into the house and had to ask the servants what was going on in there.

There are people who attend church every Sunday and are part of ministry, but they don't have a clue as to what's going on—what God is doing, where He is taking the church, or where they fit into that. The prodigal son went out, turned away from his family and home, and returned, but the elder son is the sad one in the story because he lived all that time in the house—he ate there and slept there, but he didn't know what was going on.

"Working It Out" –God's Way

And so it's important that we get that understanding from the head to the heart. The heart is where we believe. Where faith begins. We need to believe what we hear.

We need to say to ourselves: "I believe what God has spoken to me. I embrace it, and I lean my life completely on it. It's going to govern me. It's going to guide me. It's going to lead me. I trust Him implicitly. I put my life in His hands."

Head knowledge first, then heart knowledge. God works in us to will and to do His good pleasure, but remember the admonition: "Work out your own salvation." Now you've got to move all that you know and believe God has spoken to you—all the dreams, all the things that He has deposited in you—from your head to your heart.

Now you have to get to the place where you work it out. To what we call "hand knowledge."

Those are the three H's: head knowledge, heart knowledge, and hand knowledge. That simply means that now it is working out in my life. What good is it for me to know Genesis through Revelation, to be able quote all the Scriptures, to say that I trust Christ, if I can't work it out in my relationship with my own mate? Or I can't work it out in my own relationship as a single person? Or I can't work it out in my relationship with my kids or where I live?

What good is it if it's just locked up in us?

Scripture says, "Work out your own salvation with fear and trembling." We've got to get the knowledge from simple belief to action so that we can see the will of God being done in our life, in our relationships, in all of our activities.

What good is it for me to be saved if I'm broke all the time, if I can't manage my money? What good is it for me to be saved if I am always depressed, always feeling lonely, dejected, like I'm not good enough, feeling like I'm an outcast?

Jesus says you will know the truth, and the truth will do something for you: it will set you free. What good is knowing the truth if you aren't living it? What good is saying, "Man, I know God can do anything. I know God can break this depression. I know God can break this cycle of poverty. I know God can work this out . . . ," if it doesn't set you free to receive and embrace everything that God has for you?

We live, as believers, too far beneath our privileges as the sons and daughters of God.

However, everyone "works it out" differently. You can go to anyone and ask, "How can I work out my salvation?" They might tell you, "Here's how to work out your own salvation. You know, first you have to go to church, and then you pray, you must sing this praise song, and then you should pray fifteen minutes as a family, followed by fifteen minutes of worship and praise, now fifteen minutes of warfare . . ." If we copy what others do, we only become cookie-cutter Christians.

Some may walk into church with the same suit, the same hat, the same dress—but each is an entirely different person. Some people are demonstrative. Some people are energetic. Some people are quiet. It's so important that we understand just who we ourselves are.

I need to know how God made *me*. How God designed *me*. What my makeup is like, and who I am in Christ.

We need to each recognize that we are special and unique with Him. It's important that we understand that.

I saw a Peanuts cartoon strip one time. It showed Charlie Brown having a conversation with Lucy about purpose in life—a big, deep discussion. Lucy says, "You know, Charlie Brown, life is like a deck chair. Some place the chair so that they can see where they're going, and some place it so that they can see where they've been. And some place it so that they can see where they are in the present. Life's like a deck chair, and you have to position it to understand the purpose of it." And Charlie Brown says, "Aw, man, I can't even get mine unfolded."

Sometimes we feel like that, don't we? We'd like to understand our past, we'd like to understand where we're going, and we'd like to understand our present, but we can't even get it unfolded.

However, when we learn how to distinguish God's voice from all others, we will know just how to not only "unfold" our life but also know the exact place to position ourselves to be all God purposed us to be.

Chapter 2: Distinguishing God's Voice from All Others

The question I've heard more than any other as I've traveled and pastored is "What is the will of God for me?" They add, "I just wish I knew the will of God for my life . . ."

So many people seem to be searching for the will of God that we might think that God was hiding His will the way parents hide Easter eggs. As if it's a game of "hot and cold."

"No . . . you're getting hotter, hotter, no, now you're cold, cold, colder . . ." But why would God hide His will from us like that?

Paul said, essentially: "I've finished my course. I found my purpose! Got on with it, I completed it, I'm ready" (2 Tim. 4:7). Jesus said, "I did what you asked me to do. I finished the work that you gave me to do" (John 17:4 paraphrased).

The truth is, God isn't hiding His will from us at all. He doesn't want us spending our lives wondering about our divine purpose. The real issue is we have a hard time *hearing* and *distinguishing* the voice of God.

Have you ever wondered, "Was that the Lord? Was that me? Or was that the Devil?" We question His voice instead of learning to discern it and embrace it.

One reason we have this problem is that we have so many voices in our lives. We've got the radio, we've got YouTube, we've got television, we've got kids, we've got a spouse, we've got friends, we've got family, we've got newspapers, we've got society—all these voices are speaking, and it's hard for us to distinguish God's voice. And that's why we have a difficult time discovering the will of God—because we are tuned in to too many stations.

Get Alone with God

We need time, then, to withdraw ourselves and get alone with God.

When Jesus rose from the dead and was in the garden, Mary saw Him and said "Rabboni," and she ran and clung to Him. But Jesus told her, "Do not cling to Me, for I have not yet ascended to my Father" (John 20:17 NKJV). And that's what we have to do with life sometimes. We have to say, "Stop clinging to me. The best thing I can do for this situation, the best thing I can do for you, the best thing I can do for my children, is to go to the Father."

The best thing I can do is get alone with God, and then I will be able to fulfill whatever it is I need to do in this given circumstance.

Jesus had a mother, Jesus had an earthly father, Jesus had brothers, Jesus had a job as a carpenter, Jesus had responsibilities. When He started His ministry, He was thirty years old. Jesus had to deal with people who didn't receive Him. He had to deal with rejection. He had to listen to [the voices of the Roman government and the Pharisees and the Sadducees and the religious community of that day. Jesus had to listen to all the questions from His disciples and from His friends, such as Mary and

Martha. He was surrounded by all these competing voices.

But you see Jesus withdrawing many times to spend time alone with God—so that He could stand and say, as He did in John 8:29 (NKJV), "I always do those things that please [the Father]." Well, how do you know what pleases Him? By spending time with Him. And if Jesus needed to spend time with Him, how much more true is that for us?

Take a look at what Jesus says at Mark 7:31–35 (NKJV):

> Departing from the region of Tyre and Sidon, He came through the midst of the region of Decapolis to the Sea of Galilee. Then they brought to Him one who was deaf and had an impediment in his speech, and they begged Him to put His hand on him. And He took him aside from the multitude and put His fingers in his ears, and He spat and touched his tongue. Then, looking up to heaven, He sighed and said to him, 'Ephphatha,' that is, 'be opened.' Immediately his ears were opened, and the impediment of his tongue was loosed, and he spoke plainly.

The word I want you to pull out of this story is *Ephphatha*. It means "to be open." And that's the key to hearing God's voice. "Be open."

We Have to Be Open to Hear God

Note that when Jesus was passing through the Decapolis, His disciples brought over to Him a man who was deaf. People who are deaf can't hear. They can't receive verbal communication. Communication is a two-way street. You have a receiver, and you have a sender. You must be able to receive in order to communicate effectively, and you must be able to send to communicate effectively.

Spiritually, this man had no receiver. He couldn't get tuned in. He wasn't getting clear communication.

Then the Scripture says he had an impediment in his speech. He could not express himself verbally because of this impediment. He had problems not only with his receiver but with conveying what he wanted to say. People who are deaf and dumb, or have an impediment of speech, do not have the ability to communicate clearly.

Likewise, spiritually, there are times when we don't know how to hear from God or understand how God speaks to us, and we can't effectively communicate what it is that God has deposited in us. We don't have a clear pathway to send or receive.

We Shouldn't Resort to "Sign Language"

What happens when people are spiritually deaf and dumb? Just as with people who are literally deaf and dumb: they resort to sign language. Now, for the physically deaf and dumb, sign language is a wonderful gift and way to communicate. But for the believer, being reduced to "sign language" keeps us at a level of immaturity. We're always looking for a sign.

"What's the will of God? I'm going to wait until an angel comes into my room, and the lights flash on and off, and I hear, 'Hello, Tony, I want you to go down three blocks to Sixth Street, and you'll see a man with a blue T-shirt on and jeans. I want you to tell him about me.'"

When we're reduced to sign language, we believe we have to *feel something*. When we are reduced to sign language, then we're always looking for a word. Let any speaker come through, I can guarantee you, there'll be a line out that door if he's coming to give a word to the church. "Oh, do you have a word for *me* from the Lord?"

"Yea, the Lord says . . . and the Lord's going to use you—lift up your hands. I'm going to anoint those hands. God's going to . . ."

We want a sign. We're looking for a word from everyone else. But not from God.

God Talks to You Directly

God talks to you every day; you talk to Him every day. He knows you better than anyone else. So why would He send someone to tell you what to do if you're in communication and relationship with Him?

You can't govern your life by outward signs; you must govern your life upon your relationship and your ability to hear from God by His Spirit in your own heart.

Yes, sometimes you'll get confirmations and outward signs of some sort. Yes, there are times when the prophetic comes. But if someone prophesies and tells me to quit my job and go to Brazil to work for the next three years, and I've got four kids and a mortgage and a pile of bills, am I really supposed to quit my job that day and go? See, if God hasn't been speaking to me, how am I going to let someone else come in and give me a prophetic word that's going to uproot my whole life?

God doesn't deal with us like that. He's been confirming and preparing you all along, but if you do get a prophetic utterance or word of knowledge, it only *confirms* what God through His Word and your relationship with Him in prayer has already been preparing you for.

Getting Alone with God

Mark 7:33 says something important that we must catch hold of. It says, "He took [a man who was deaf] aside from the multitude." Isn't that amazing? When God really wants to talk to us, He will pull us aside. And that's a key to your walk with Jesus Christ—to learn how to be alone with God.

David learned that secret. That's what made David such a great king, warrior, and shepherd. That's what made David such a great psalmist. That's what made David such a great lover of God. He knew how to be alone with God.

The Bible gives us insight into David's secret. He had no one to talk to. He had no one to hang with. When he was on the hillsides of Judea, out there by himself watching his father's flock, he didn't have a radio or CD player. Didn't have anyone he could ask, "Hey, was that God talking to me? What do you think?" He couldn't ask his sheep, so he could only talk to God.

And when he was alone with God, when things got tough, he had only God to rely on. When the bear came, he defeated the bear. When the lion came, he defeated the lion. Alone with God.

So when faced with Goliath, it was no big deal. He told King Saul, essentially, "I was alone with God and defeated the lion. I was alone with God and defeated the bear. This uncircumcised Philistine will be like one of them, because he has defied the armies of the living God. The Lord who rescued me from the paw of the lion and the paw of the bear will rescue me from the hand of this Philistine" (1 Sam. 17:34–36). And he defeated the thing that stood in the way of Israel accomplishing what God had purposed them to do.

Spending time alone with God was Jesus's way to hear God's voice. He always made time to be alone with God. Always. He would finish preaching and go be alone with God.

Peter and James and John would go looking for Him, and they would ask, "Where you were?" Jesus would tell them, "I was up on the mountain. Go ahead. I'll catch up with you later." And then He would go to a secret place and pray.

When God takes us aside, we are developed and we mature more than at any other time in our lives. More than any teaching is going to give you, more than any church service is going to do for you. The time you spend alone with God is the most valuable time you will ever spend in your life.

Remember how Jesus took the deaf and dumb man aside and put His fingers in his ears? That's significant because He put His fingers in the man's ears. Because Jesus wanted him to learn how to hear not with his physical ears but with his heart. "He that hath an ear, let him hear what the spirit says unto the churches" (Rev. 2:7 KJV). When God speaks to our heart, we must learn how to get it *past our ears*. Hear it not in our head but in our heart.

Spit Out the Things That Keep You from Hearing God's Voice

Then Jesus puts His fingers in the man's ears, and He spits.

How spiritual can spitting be? You spit when you want to get rid of something that's in your mouth. Something you don't want. And there are times when we need to spit out of our lives things, such as close-mindedness and things that limit us. Those spiritual ceilings we have covering our lives that keep us in this little box we're in. There are fears that need to be disposed of. There are doubts that we need to get rid of.

We say, "Well, I can't do that," and "I can only go so far," and "God would never use me to do this," and all the things that you've heard other people tell you—saying that you're not good at this or that. You need to get rid of those things.

And so Jesus spits. He doesn't have the man spit; Jesus spits. Then it says that He touched the man's tongue. Touched his tongue in order to impart life, His own DNA. The tongue is the organ of speech, and now Jesus puts life in the man's tongue. And then Jesus looks up to heaven, and He sighs.

I wonder how many times Jesus sighs over us. Has the Lord ever given you something to do, and you get confused and say, "I'm not going to do this" or "I'm not really sure of what you really want me to do."

Here you are—one of God's people—and you're frustrated. God's empowered you, the Holy Spirit is residing within you, you are involved in a great ministry, you're free, you're saved, you're Holy Spirit baptized and filled, and here you are bound and limited to sign language and not doing anything.

I think of the times that Jesus looks at me and sighs. "If only you knew what I want to do with you. If only you understood who I am. If only you realized the potential that I have deposited in you. If only you knew the gift of God that resides within you. If only you knew whose presence you are in. If only you understood the will and the purpose of God and that even though you don't have the strength or the energy to fulfill it, I will supply even that."

He sighs, and He says these words: "Ephphatha. Ephphatha. Be open. Be open."

"Be Open"

He speaks not only to our ears but to our hearts. "Don't get so locked in; don't be so limited. Be open."

Be open to God. Open to what God wants to do through you. Open to the way that God wants to use you. Open to God to provide for you. Open for God to instruct you.

When God instructs us, He builds structure in us. The word *con*struction speaks of the outer building structure. But when you *in*struct, it's about building structure on the inside. God wants to instruct you and to build structure on the inside.

If we don't learn how to be open, we're going to limit God. See, once we understand and learn how to hear the voice of God, if we limit God to only speaking to us through the Word, or only speaking to us when we are in prayer, do you know how limited that makes us? If we believe the only time God speaks to us is when we are in the Word, we are in trouble. Because we're not in the Word all the time. If the only time God speaks to us is when we are in prayer, again, we're in trouble.

When you are open, God can speak to you from the back of a cornflakes box. God can speak to you through a game or while you're watching a movie or talking with a friend.

Be open to hearing from God twenty-four hours a day.

Now, you always want to run what you hear through the Word of God to make sure to filter out anything that's not aligned with God. But God can inspire you, God can speak to you, anytime when you are open to Him.

We can be open to Him in every area of our life. How we design our bedroom, so that when we go in we feel comfortable and we get rest. What kind of paintings we want in our house. What kind of music we want to listen to. What kind of food we're going eat.

I can be open for God to design everything. My marriage as well as the people I hang out with. Open to allowing God to design my friendships.

Take away the ceiling and say, "Okay, God, whatever you want to do, I'm open. Holy Spirit, you guide me, you lead me, you help me; I'm open."

Part II: Five Openings

In order to hear God's voice and know what His plans are for our life, we need to be spiritually open. The twenty-fourth chapter of Luke gives us insight into five ways we must be open in order to understand our divine design and unlock the door to God's purpose for our life.

Chapter 3: The First Opening—Victory

The first opening we need to learn about is
victory. Christ was victorious over the grave, and as a
result, he's given us victory. We must embrace that
victory to experience and work out God's design for
our lives. Let's take a look at a passage in Scripture
that explains this opening.

> Now on the first day of the week, very early in
> the morning, they and certain other women came
> to the tomb bringing spices which they had
> prepared. But they found the stone rolled away
> from the tomb. Then they went in and did not
> find the body of the Lord Jesus. (Luke 24:1–3
> NKJV)

The first opening is symbolized by *the open tomb*.
The tomb was not opened so that Jesus could get out.
The tomb was opened so that *we* could get *in* and see
that it was empty. So we could see the victory that
belonged to us. Jesus rose from the dead in victory
and provides this victory to those who belong to
Him.

Paul says: "O death, where is thy sting; O grave,
where is thy victory?" (1 Cor. 15:55 KJV). First and
foremost, the open tomb is God's receipt to you for
victory. The first opening signifies the victory that is
ours in Jesus. Open yourself to victory in every single

area of your life. Don't keep saying, "Oh, I just was born like this. I'll never change. I can't make a difference. I can't do this."

Be open to victory in the areas in which you are experiencing defeat or areas that you are finding hard.

We all have areas in our life—whether it's our temper, whether it's uncontrolled desires, whether it's one thing or another—in which things seem to conquer us.

Open up, first, for your victory over sin and death.

Be open to the truth that Satan was the usurper of the authority God gave to man. The Bible says, "The earth is the Lord's and all its fullness" (Psalm 24:1), and Genesis 1:1 says, "In the beginning God created the heavens and the earth." So the earth belongs to the Lord.

But God, in His goodness, gave dominion to man. Psalm 115:16 (NIV) says, "The highest heavens belong to the Lord, but the earth he has given to mankind."

However, man transferred that dominion through an act of disobedience to God, and Satan then became the prince of this world. Four times in the gospel of John Jesus says, "The prince of this world has come and has found nothing in me." Judgment has come, and it is time for the prince of this world to be judged (John 16:11).

"Make Me!"

Jesus acknowledges that Satan is the prince of this world. He has stolen from man his authority and his dominion. Jesus Christ came as a man to regain dominion. And Christ did, on Calvary. Christ died, and when He rose from the dead, victory was provided to us.

The problem is, Satan won't acknowledge our victory. He's stubborn.

Did you ever play shoot-'em-up cowboys when you were a kid and say to your friend, "Okay, you're shot," and he answers, "No I'm not—you missed"? Or he loses in checkers and says, "Well, let's do best four out of seven." And when he keeps losing, he says, "Best eleven out of twenty." He refuses to acknowledge that he's been defeated.

Well, Satan also refuses to acknowledge that he has been defeated. So when you stand and say, "I am a believer; Satan, get behind me." He says, "Make me."

As funny as that sounds, that's what we have to do. We have to make him. We can't waste time trying to reason with him. "Aw, come on, now, you know you're defeated by the blood of Jesus. Let me show you this verse . . ."

We have to come determined and confident. We have to come ready for battle. The victory belongs to us. It is ours. We must, through prayer and through the Word of God, take what is ours. But if we're not open to victory, we let Satan run roughshod over our lives.

God has a people on the earth who are living out the truth that Christ is victorious. God wants to get glory out of our lives, as we are to take back territory that the Devil has stolen.

And so you must be open to God's victory. Don't give in, saying, "I can't get victory in that area."

Be open to the victory that has been bought and paid for over every area of your life.

We must first get victory over ourselves. We are our own biggest problem. Then we need to be open for victory over "problem people" we are dealing with. Open for victory over our finances. Open for victory over loneliness and depression and things that we wrestle with on any given day.

Be open for victory in any circumstance you are facing. Yes, God *can* manifest victory right where you are. That's the first opening that will start to unlock the door to discovering God's purpose for your life.

Chapter 4: The Second Opening—Your Eyes

After Jesus was crucified, two of His disciples were on the road to Emmaus (Luke 24:13–35). Jesus joined them, but they didn't recognize Him. Verse 16 says, "But their eyes were holden that they should not know Him" (KJV). The Hebrew word for *holden* means to keep in check, restrain, to hold back. Not until He came into the house with them, took bread, blessed it, broke it, and gave it to them, did they suddenly realize who He was. Their eyes were opened. Jesus kept them from seeing who He really was until the moment He chose to open their eyes and reveal Himself.

There is a process in having your eyes opened, and this is shown by Jesus's taking of bread. Every time you see bread in the hands of the Lord in Scripture, He is either taking it, blessing it, breaking it, or giving it.

Every person that God takes in His hands goes through the same process. Either you're in the process of God taking you from one place to another, or you're being blessed by God, or you're being broken by Him, or you're being given by Him.

God took Abraham, then He blessed him. He broke him at Mt. Moriah, and He gave him to be the father of the nation of Israel.

Look at David. God took him from following the sheep, then He blessed him with the anointing to be king. God then broke David through problems and difficulties in life, and then He gave him to Israel as their greatest king and psalmist.

Look at the apostle Paul. God took him; blessed him with revelation of Jesus; broke him through shipwrecks, beatings, rejection, prison—all manner of suffering—then gave him as a great apostle to the nations.

But our greatest example is Jesus Christ Himself. God took Him from heaven. He was blessed more than anyone who ever walked the face of the earth. God broke Him at Calvary, and then God gave Him as Lord and Savior to all of us.

We are all at some stage in that process. When we understand that, we recognize that there are times God is breaking us because we're too full of ourselves. There are times He "*gives* us as a blessing to others." There are times He blesses us. There are times He moves or takes us somewhere either physically or spiritually.

After Jesus took bread and blessed and broke it, He gave it to His disciples. And what followed was "their eyes were opened, and they knew Him, and He vanished out of their sight" (verse 31).

Christ Comes to Open Our Eyes

The first opening is victory. The second is the opening of our eyes so that we can know Him. We've been blinded, Paul tells us, by the god of this world (2 Cor. 4:4). And Christ comes to open our eyes.

God's in the eye business. When Balaam was going the way of disobedience on his donkey, he didn't know what in the world was going on. His donkey could see it, but he couldn't. So, finally, God opened his eyes, and Balaam saw an angel with a sword blocking his way (Num. 22:21–35).

We need to pray, "God, open our eyes so that we don't end up way over here when you desire us to be way over there. Open our eyes so we can see when we are treading in dangerous places."

Remember Hagar, Sarah's servant? In the desert, she's about to die, ready to give up her life, but God opens her eyes and she sees a well. And she is refreshed (Gen. 21:19). There are times when we feel all alone, but when God opens our eyes, we are able to find the refreshment we need.

One morning Elijah's servant runs inside their home and tells Elijah, "Listen, the armies have surrounded us." Elijah tells him, "They that are with us are more than they that are against us." Then he prays, "Lord, open his eyes." God opens the servant's eyes and shows him the mountains full of horses and chariots of fire surrounding Elijah. (2 Kings 6:14–17).

Our eyes need to be open to see all the help that God has provided for us. "Their eyes were opened and they knew Him." God reveals Himself to us. That's why Christianity never gets old—because Jesus is continually unfolding Himself to us. Continually revealing Himself to us.

The Ways God Reveals Himself to Us

First, He reveals Himself as Savior. He's the savior of our soul. Then He reveals Himself as Deliverer. He delivers us from whatever we need to be delivered from. Then, if we're sick, He can come and reveal Himself as Healer. He is able to heal our bodies. Heal our memories. Heal our hurts. Heal us in every way.

We must be open to Him to be a provider. We can pray, "God, I have a need—please provide." Then reveals Himself to us as Provider.

There are times when we need a friend. What a precious season that is in our life, when we realize that Jesus is our friend. That He cares about us.

There are times when you need a miracle in your life. If you're open, then He will reveal Himself to you as a miracle-worker. When you're between a rock and a hard place, remember that God made the rock and He made the hard place—and He can make a door leading out of anywhere.

He's food for the hungry. He's light for those who are in darkness. He's strength for the weak. Scripture says when Jesus opened those two disciples' eyes, they *knew Him*. Do you know Him as Savior? Do you know Him as Way-Maker? Do you know Him as Provider? Do you know Him as Healer? Do you know Him as a counselor? Do you know Him as a friend?

He wants to reveal Himself to you. That's the awesome thing about God. That's why our relationship with Christ never gets old, because every day He can reveal Himself in new ways.

In Isaiah and in Revelation, the angels in heaven cry, "Holy, holy, holy" without ceasing. God gave me a picture in my heart one day, showing that the angels have been there for millions of years, and yet God is continuing to unfold Himself. And with each amazing revelation, their response is awe and wonder. He never runs out of ways to unfold Himself. Every day, His mercies are fresh.

We should have that same kind of excitement. We should wonder, "How are you going to reveal yourself today, Jesus? I'm in a jam. I don't know what I'm going to do. But my eyes are on you. I'm excited to see how you going to reveal yourself in my life today."

So to hear God's voice and direction for our lives, our eyes must be open. They must be on Him, turned to Him, gazing at Him.

Chapter 5: The Third Opening—The Scriptures

After Jesus opened the two disciples' eyes on the road to Emmaus, the Bible tells us: "And they said to one another, 'Did not our heart burn within us while He talked with us on the road, and while He opened the scriptures to us?'" (Luke 24:32 NKJV)

So, in addition to being open to victory, with eyes open, God also desires for us to be open to the Scriptures. When our eyes are open to His Word, we see who He is. But not only do the Scriptures reveal who He is, they also reveal *who we are*.

Not only do we get to know who He is, we get to understand who we are in Him. That we are sons and daughters of God. We are honored and rewarded—not by what we do but by who we are.

Be open to the truth that you are the righteousness of God in Christ Jesus. It took me a long time to be open to that. "Me, the righteousness of God?"

But that's how He sees us. Through the Scriptures we understand that we are kings and priests, and that we are to reign with Him.

Authority in Christ

When we are open to the Scriptures, we understand that we have authority in Christ. When Jesus asked the demons inhabiting the man in

Gadarenes, "What's your name?" the demon did not give Jesus a proper name. Instead he said, "Legion, for we are many." He told Jesus the *authority* by which he held that man bound. Well, Jesus replied, essentially, "My authority's greater than that. Come out." And the demons had to recognize His authority and freed the man.

So when we say "In the name of Jesus," we are invoking the authority of Jesus Christ. We must understand our authority in Him. He told His disciples that they "will be able to handle snakes with safety, and if they drink anything poisonous, it won't hurt them. They will be able place their hands on the sick and they will be healed" (Mark 16:18 NLT).

We understand this authority we've been given when the Scriptures are open to us. We understand the covenant that we have with Christ. That this is a new covenant—not an old covenant based on the Law but one based on the finished work of Calvary. It's based on what He did. It's based on who He is.

A covenant is an agreement. You've got to do your part; I've got to do my part. As long as we're keeping up our end of the bargain, we're fine. Have you ever made an agreement with a friend and you say something like, "I'll lend you fifty dollars, but I need it back by Friday," and he comes back with twenty—a day late and thirty dollars short? That wasn't the agreement! Your friend broke the covenant.

When God created man, He made a covenant with him. But when Adam sinned, he broke that covenant. Later, God instituted a covenant with Abraham and his descendants, and through Moses gave the Law and the commandments. But humans could never keep such a perfect law. They failed to uphold their part of the covenant. The Bible says, "All our righteous acts are like filthy rags" (Isa. 64:6 NIV) and "All have sinned and fall short of the glory of God" (Rom. 3:23 NKJV). So the old covenant never worked because of the weakness of man.

Was the problem with the covenant? No. The problem was with the flesh. Not with God's Word. It was because we could never quite measure up that God, in His infinite mercy, became a man. Not only did He fulfill His part of the covenant, He fulfilled *our* part of the covenant as well. And that makes it the new covenant.

We need to understand from the Scriptures our covenant with Him. That we are in a covenant because He did it all. And because He did it all, we come to understand that we are "more than conquerors through Him that loved us" (Rom. 8:37).

When we are open to the victory obtained by Jesus, with our eyes open to who God is and how He views us, we must delve into the Scriptures and be open to what they tell us about our place and purpose in God's will. But it's not enough to be open to the Scriptures; we also must be open to the understanding God reveals to us.

Chapter 6: The Fourth Opening—Understanding

Remember the key word here? Ephphatha. Be open. "He opened their *understanding* that they might comprehend the scriptures." Understanding is crucial. When we are open, we are no longer confused; we now have understanding.

The Bible says, "Wisdom is the principal thing; Therefore, get wisdom. And in all of your getting, get understanding" (Prov. 4:7 NKJV).

When we're open, we begin to understand each other. We begin to understand the ways of God. We begin to understand the trials that we go through. We begin to understand the problems that we are facing. We begin to understand who we are in Him. Who He is. We begin to understand our victory. We begin to understand the timing of God in our lives.

We also begin to understand the seasons of God in our lives. Sometimes it's summer; sometimes it's winter. If you understand that it's wintertime, you wrap up and hang tight, because this is a season in your life. When it's summer, and God is blessing you, you go out and believe God for everything you can. You embrace everything that God has for you because, I guarantee you, winter's coming. There are going to be times when you can't feel God. So when you wake up and wonder where God is, you recall in your heart the goodness of God. Our faith is enhanced and energized by remembering what God has done for us. That's all part of understanding.

You're not always going to be on the mountaintop. You're not always going to be skipping into the sanctuary. You're not always going to be singing, "Praise the Lord, hallelujah." Sometimes you're going to be sad and down.

But when you understand who He is, your circumstances do not take control and seize your life and dictate who you are and who you aren't.

You say, "This is a tough time I'm going through, but God is faithful. He's still on the throne. I belong to Him. I am His son [or daughter]. I am an ambassador of Christ. I still have a responsibility as a priest and a king, regardless of what I'm feeling and what I'm going through, to minister to Him and to fulfill what He has called me to do."

The Unpredictableness of God

Sometimes God just doesn't make sense. We'll look at what God is doing in our life and say, "I don't get it, you know? Why all this? Just send the money!" or "Just work it out; what's the problem? Why do I have to change a flat tire on the freeway when it's raining and cold, and I have a trunk full of stuff that I have to set on the side before I can get to the spare tire? I don't need this! I don't need to be late for work. I don't need this traffic. I don't need this drama in my life. I don't need this kid of mine getting an attitude with me. God, fix it!"

When we understand the ways of God, the timing and the seasons of God, we know that life is going to bring some unusual circumstances. Knowing that, we open up to the unexpectedness of God.

God never does the same thing twice. There are no two snowflakes that are exactly alike. There are no two drops of water that are identical. There are no two grains of sand that are the same. He never repeats Himself. He's a God of variety.

When we understand that, we say "God, come any way you want."

We're looking at one door for God to come in through, but when we are open, when our understanding is open, we say, "God, come any way you want. Come through the ceiling; come through the door. You know, if you want to send a raven with the money, fine." Sometimes He says, "Open the paper and look at the Want Ads for a job. I'll supply you when you go to work!"

Elijah prayed to die, and God told him, "No, you're going to live." Moses prayed to live, and God said, "No, you're going to die."

God called the apostle Paul into ministry, who was a brilliant Pharisee who knew all about Judaism and the Law. You'd think God would use him to reach educated Jews with the gospel, but instead He sent him to the Gentiles, who didn't know a thing about Judaism. And God took an uneducated fisherman like Peter, who had never been to school, and sent him to preach to the Jews. What kind of stuff is this?

Paul goes to prison; Peter goes to prison. When Paul goes to prison, God shakes the whole prison down. Walls fall down, chains fall off, and he gets out of prison due to a big earthquake. In Peter's case,

God sends an angel and quietly slips Peter out of the prison.

If Peter had been closed to God's ways, he might have said, "God, I'm not moving until you send an earthquake. I want an earthquake just like Paul had." And he'd have been so busy waiting for that earthquake, he wouldn't have noticed the angel tugging on his shirt.

Be Open to Prophecy

We also need to be open to understanding prophecy. Sometimes the prophetic happens instantly; other times it takes years. Jesus passed a fig tree, spoke to it and cursed it, and it was dried up the next day when he came back. Jesus spoke prophetically about the temple, and decades later the Roman general Titus destroyed the temple, fulfilling Jesus's words that not one stone would be left upon another.

Some prophecy is fulfilled now; some later. We have to understand this. And when we accept God's unpredictability, we are set free. We can say, "I recognize you are a God of creativity. I'm not going to dictate how you are going to deliver me. I'm not going to dictate how you're going to provide for me. But, Lord, I'm just looking for you to provide. I'm open. Whatever you want."

We're so spiritual that we miss simple things God is doing. When you think of a rock, what comes to mind? You might think of "Jesus, the rock of our salvation." We're built on the rock. But some guy was kicking a rock, and he thought, "Hey, why don't I put these in boxes and call them Pet Rocks?" and made a million dollars.

Many times creativity has been stymied in the church—regarding the ways we can reach people for Christ or the ways that we can worship God. We become so limited. Remember the woman at Jesus's feet? She broke the alabaster box; she took her hair and began to wash Jesus's feet. No one had ever worshiped God in that manner. True worship is spontaneous. She let her hair down, signifying that she was taking a worshipful stance, and she wept and she worshiped the Lord. She gave all that she had.

Her alabaster box didn't have a cap on it to allow her to pour just a little perfume out. She had to break the box to release the perfume.

Sometimes we dole out tiny portions of worship, like drops of perfume. That's how we worship the Lord. Here's a little this Sunday. Here's another drop Wednesday night at Bible study. Now we put the box back into storage.

But the woman at Jesus's feet had to break the box. That's why Judas was so angry. That perfume cost a year's wages. Today that might amount to forty, fifty, or one hundred thousand dollars. Jesus says, "Leave this woman alone. What she did will be a testimony wherever the gospel is preached." She didn't have any preconceived notion of how to worship. She was open to the leading of her heart. Open to God's leading.

In our worship, we shouldn't get locked into religious rites or tradition, or crammed into any mold. God is a God of variety. Just look at the kinds of worship ministries that have sprung up in churches—drama, and mime, dance and plays. The arts now are celebrated and a way to give glory and honor to God. There is no limit.

God is so big, so why would we be narrow-minded in our worship? He only requires that, when we worship Him, we worship Him in spirit and in truth. That's the only requirement.

Examples of Those Who Were Open to God

Take a look at Joseph's life. God gave him this wonderful promise of future glory through powerful dreams , but Joseph had to remain open to how God brought this promise to fruition. Joseph had to remain open when his brothers sold him into slavery. He had to remain open in Potiphar's house. He had to remain open in prison. He had to remain open everywhere he went. He knew what his gifting was, and he was open for God to use it. He was not a prophet. He was not a king. He was not a seer. Yes, he was given the gift of interpreting dreams, but Joseph's gift was primarily in administration.

So his brothers threw him in a pit, and he ended up sold to Potiphar in Egypt. What does he do? He administrates. He gets falsely accused and kicked out of Potiphar's house and thrown into prison. What does he do? He administrates. He gets put in charge of all the prisoners during the two years he's in jail. Then, when God wants to use him, he's got him right where He wants. He's been preparing Joseph for years for the big job. What does He use him to do? To administrate Egypt's food for the saving of a whole nation.

If Joseph wasn't open to understanding God's ways, he'd have given up when he hit the pit. But Joseph knew God had His hand on his life, and so he said to his brothers, when they later admitted their sin in throwing him in a pit, "It wasn't you that put me here. It was God. You meant it for evil, but see, I understand that God's bigger than whatever you meant. He meant it for good" (Gen. 50:20 paraphrased).

Then there's Moses. Look at his life. He grew up in Pharaoh's house. He was raised like royalty. He knew all the court procedures, witnessed everything that went on in Egyptian history for forty years. Then God took him to the back side of the desert and broke him. Then He gave him back to Israel as a great deliverer. Who else would have known how to approach Pharaoh? Who else would have known how to go in and say, "God says, 'Let my people go'"? Moses stayed open for eighty years of his life and then began to be used by God in the most awesome way that he ever experienced.

Take Esther. What was Esther's great gift? She was beautiful. See, if you're beautiful, you can work that beauty for the glory of God. Because she was beautiful—more beautiful than anyone else—she was able to get into the king's house to be in position in her life, because she was open. Her cousin Mordecai said to her, "Who knows if God brought you and placed you here for such a time as this?" (Est. 4:14). God positioned Esther to bring about the salvation of nine million Jews. And He used her beauty to do it.

Daniel is another great example. He never compromised. Though he was a prophet, his greatest work that he did in the earth was as an advisor. When taken into captivity to Babylon as a young man, he became a personal advisor to Nebuchadnezzar, and he continued this position for seven other kings who ruled Babylon and Persia over the course of seventy years. He trusted God through those gifts. And God delivered him time after time, from the lion's den and from everything else he faced. But he had to remain open to what God called him to do and how God could use him. He, like Joseph, could have given up, thrown up his hands when he was in the pit. He could have complained, "God, I did everything you asked me to do. I stood, I prayed, I refused to worship other gods, and now I've been thrown to the lions? I see where prayer gets you." But instead, he remained open and eventually he understood.

Consider Joseph of Arimathea. God made him rich for a reason—so that he could purchase and provide the tomb in which Christ would be laid. But if he had not been rich, he wouldn't have owned the tomb, and God couldn't have used Joseph to fulfill a prophecy uttered seven hundred years earlier (Isa. 53:9).

Paul's nephew is another example of someone who was open to God. Not much is known in Scripture about him; we don't even know his name. But he overheard men tell the chief priests that they had taken an oath stating that they would not eat or sleep until they had killed Paul (Acts 23:16). I wonder if those guys died from that oath they took because they never killed him. But he was in the right place at the right time, in position and open for God to use him. The nephew went to the barracks where Paul was being held and told him about the plot. Paul told the soldier to take his nephew to the commander, who listened to the boy's report. The commander then slipped Paul out of town early and delivered him safely to Felix, the governor.

When we're closed to God and how He might act in our lives, we limit Him. Psalm 78:41 says, "they limited the Holy One of Israel." Did you know that you can limit God? Because His people limited the Holy One of Israel, He could do nothing on their behalf. It's not that God can't, but God will not cross our will.

How do you limit God? Through unbelief.

The Bible says that when Lazarus died, Jesus wept. He wept over Jerusalem too (John 11:35; Luke 19:41). Why would Jesus weep? Why would you cry if you know you are getting ready to go raise a man up from the dead? Tears for what? God's getting ready to be glorified, so why would He cry?

The only time you cry is when something is out of your control. You don't cry if you're hungry and you have bologna and cheese in the fridge and bread in the cupboard! It would be silly to cry. All you have to do is go make a sandwich. You don't cry over that. You cry when it is out of your control.

So what made Jesus cry? Mary's and Martha's unbelief. He was *hurt* by their unbelief. Why did He cry over Jerusalem? He said, "How often I have longed to gather your children together . . . and you were not willing" (Matt. 23:37 NKJV). He wept because they would not trust in Him. *Because of their unbelief.* He could do nothing about their unbelief. Because that's the freedom that God gave to us.

Either we trust Him or we don't. God will not kick down the door of your heart, grab you by the collar, pin you up against the wall, and say, "Trust me."

No, He presents Himself as He is and says, "Trust me." The choice is ours.

God is wholly dependable but wholly unpredictable. To hear His voice and know His will for our life, we must be open to His timing and His wisdom, in His way.

Understanding the Way God Delivers

If we're not open, we'll miss the way that God wants to deliver us. We'll miss the timing of God if we're not open.

Peter and John were on their way to the temple to pray, and something interrupted their prayer. A man sat at the gate begging, so they stopped and talked to him (Acts 3:1–6). If we don't understand that God wants us to put the prayer meeting on hold for a moment and minister to someone, we will miss being used by God in a great way.

We get so religious-minded that we will pass a thousand people on our way to church who are hungry and hurting. And by doing that we can miss the Lord.

Sometimes it's time to pray; sometimes it's time to minister. More than five thousand people came together to hear Jesus, but He had only two fish and five loaves of bread to satisfy their hunger. Yet, Jesus took in His hands the fish and loaves, then He blessed them, He broke them, He gave them—and five thousand were fed. In another account, four thousand were fed in like manner. Then, when on their way through Samaria, they stopped at a well. They were hot, they were tired, they were thirsty, and they were dusty. Jesus told them, "Go into town and buy some food."

You know, we probably would have said to the Lord, "Why don't you work up one of those bread miracles? It's hot out here, and it's a long way into town!" He was saying, in essence, "No, now it's time to go buy food, but there are times that I'm going to provide miraculously."

If we are not open to the way God moves, we will sit there stubbornly with our arms folded waiting for a fish-and-loaf miracle. But sometimes God says, "Go to town." Take action. Get walking.

On one occasion, to pay His taxes, Jesus leaves the money in Judas's bag; another time He tells Peter to go to the shore and catch a fish and pull the money out of a fish's mouth.

Let's not limit the ways God can provide for us. We need to be open to any avenue of deliverance. Open to understanding God's ways are not our ways, and He can come through a door any way He likes.

Jesus's Unpredictable Healing Ministry

Think about how Jesus healed during His ministry years. Sometimes He sent His word. Sometimes He touched a person. Sometimes He spit in the dirt and made mud to put on their eyes. One particular healing in Mark 7 shows Jesus putting His fingers in a man's ears and spitting on him and then touching his tongue. His disciples might have said, "Ew, why are you doing that? How come you didn't just speak the word like you did for that guy over there in Bethesda? Come on, is this really necessary?"

Jesus never healed two people the same way because people would then get locked into thinking there was only one way. Jesus shows us we need to be open to any avenue for healing. He wants us to say, "God, you can do it any way you want. I don't care. Use a doctor; use a miracle. Whatever you want to do, Lord. I am in your hands."

When we have an open understanding and we trust Him, we know that God can come in so many ways. He can tell us to go wash in the pool of Siloam; He can spit; He can send a word. He touched one man twice. Some He touched once. Blind Bartimaeus—only one touch. If we remain closed, we may miss what God wants to do.

Chapter 7: The Fifth Opening—The Heavens

The fifth and last opening spoken of in Luke 24 is found at verse 51, where Jesus is speaking one last time to His followers. "Now it came to pass, while He blessed them, He was parted from them and carried up into heaven" (NKJV).

Because of Jesus's victory over the cross, we were purchased by His blood, and so the heavens are now open to us. As sons and daughters, we can come boldly to the throne of grace and find the heavens are opened to us.

The Bible tells us that we are seated in heavenly places In Christ Jesus (Eph. 2:6).

Jesus prayed this prayer: "Thy kingdom come; thy will be done on earth as it is in heaven" (Matt. 6:10 KJV). How are we going to know how it is in heaven if we don't get insight *into* heaven? Now that we have absolute, continual, unhindered access to God, we must be open to the open heavens. That means being open to meeting with Him daily. Open to having rich fellowship and communion with Him. Open to observing heaven and God's ways.

I'm not talking about heaven as a location, because I don't know if you can locate heaven geographically. Wherever God is—that's where heaven is.

When the heavens are open, we can observe Him and have access to Him, regardless of what's going on or where we are in our life. Scripture says "Let us therefore come boldly to the throne of grace, that we may obtain mercy and find grace to help in time of need" (Heb. 4:16 NKJV). We have entrance into the very presence of God, and we've been given a seat in His presence. "There is a place by me," He told Moses (Ex. 33:21 KJV). The same thing is true for us. There is a place for us, and we are seated in heavenly places in Christ Jesus (Eph. 2:6).

The heavens are open for us to observe the ways of God. Every time we read His Word, we are privileged to look into the heavens. "In the year that King Uzziah died," Isaiah said, "I saw the Lord high and lifted up" (Isa. 6:1 NKJV). John said he was caught up into heaven and saw a throne, and he gives descriptions of what he saw there (Rev. 4:1–11). Paul relates how he was caught up into the third heaven and saw things that were not even lawful for Him to speak of (2 Cor. 12:2–4).

Well, we may not experience all that Isaiah, Paul, or John did, yet we can still have an insight into the open heavens. Even while I run errands, while I'm working, or while I'm playing ball with my grandchildren, the heavens are opened for me to observe the ways of God and to behold Him continually.

Stephen saw the heavens open up during his stoning. Peter saw it in the midst of his religious practice on a rooftop. The heavens are open during any season of our lives.

When the heavens parted and Jesus ascended, He didn't close the door behind Him. He kept it open. And just as the heavens were open to receive Him, they are open to receive us, both in this life and in the life to come.

Jesus embraces us each morning and says, "Ephphatha."

Will you be open to the victory that's yours? Will you open the eyes of your heart and let the Scriptures open to you? Will you open your understanding to the unpredictable ways of God? Will you be open to the victory that is yours in Christ Jesus? Will you be open to whatever heaven wants to do in your life?

When we are open, God can do anything with us. We get in our position—as that lump of clay. We recognize His position as the potter (Isa. 64:8). We can hear Him speak into our lives—every part. Anything can take place. Anything . . . when we are open.

About the Author

Dr. Tony Williams has served as senior pastor of Maranatha Christian Center in San Jose, California, since 1987. In 2001, he was appointed chairman of the board for Cityteam Ministry's International Committee. He is a volunteer chaplain at the Santa Clara County jail, as well as for the San Jose Police Department and volunteers at San Quentin prison.

His missionary work has taken him all over the world – from Mexico to East Africa, from the Fiji Islands to Dublin, Ireland, and numerous locales in between.

Pastor Tony currently serves on the board of directors for Cityteam Ministries. Previously he has served as a board member for the Coalition for Urban Youth Leadership, Fellowship West, Inc. (Los Angeles), and the Bay Area Billy Graham Crusade.

Dr. Williams earned a bachelor of theology from California Graduate School of Theology in Glendale, California; a master's degree in ministry and honorary doctorate of divinity from Southern California School of Ministry; a doctor of humane letters and a doctor of philosophy in Christian counseling from Vision International University.

www.ingramcontent.com/pod-product-compliance
Lightning Source LLC
Chambersburg PA
CBHW060724030426
42337CB00017B/2993